CUBISM

CUBISM

ODYSSEYS

SHANNON ROBINSON

CREATIVE EDUCATION•CREATIVE PAPERBACKS

Published by Creative Education and Creative Paperbacks
P.O. Box 227, Mankato, Minnesota 56002
Creative Education and Creative Paperbacks
are imprints of The Creative Company
www.thecreativecompany.us

Design and production by Blue Design
Art direction by Rita Marshall
Printed in the United States of America

Photographs by Art Resource, NY (Scala), Corbis (PIZZOLI
ALBERTO/CORBIS SYGMA, Jeff Albertson, Alinari Archives,
Archivo Iconografico, S.A., Bettmann, Alexander Burkatovski,
Burstein Collection, Geoffrey Clements, Corbis, Richard
Cummins, Thomas A. Heinz, Robert Holmes, Hulton-Deutsch
Collection, Charles & Josette Lenars, Francis G. Mayer, Gianni
Dagli Orti, Philadelphia Museum of Art, Bill Ross, Swim Ink)

Library of Congress Cataloging-in-Publication Data
Robinson, Shannon.
Cubism / Shannon Robinson.
p. cm. — (Odysseys in art)
Summary: An examination of the art movement known as
Cubism from its beginnings in the early 1900s to its decline
during World War I, including an introduction to great artists
and works.
Includes bibliographical references and index.
ISBN 978-1-60818-531-3 (hardcover)
ISBN 978-1-62832-132-6 (pbk)
1. Cubism—Juvenile literature. I. Title.

N6494.C8R63 2015
759.06'32—dc23   2014041719

CCSS: RI.8.1, 2, 3, 4; RI.9-10.1, 2, 3, 4; RI.11-12.1, 2, 3, 4

First Edition HC 9 8 7 6 5 4 3 2 1
First Edition PBK 9 8 7 6 5 4 3 2 1

Cover: Untitled work by Juan Gris
Page 2: *Head of a Woman (Portrait of the Artist's Mother)* by
Juan Gris (1912)
Pages 4–5: Pablo Picasso
Page 6: *Nude Descending a Staircase, No. 2* by Marcel
Duchamp (1912)

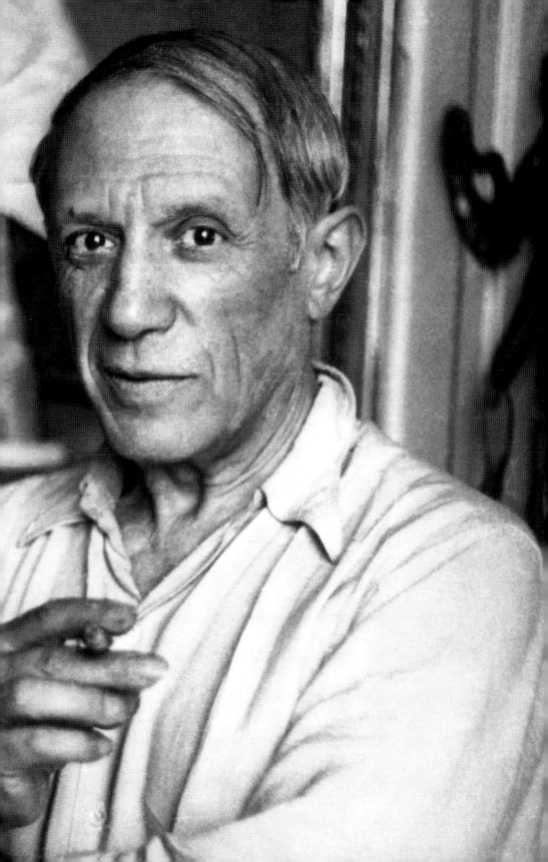

CONTENTS

Introduction

The history of the world can be told through the accounts of great battles, the lives of kings and queens, and the discoveries and inventions of scientists and explorers. But the history of the way people think and feel about themselves and the world is told through art. From paintings of the hunt in prehistoric caves, to sacred art in the European Middle Ages, to the **abstract** forms of the 20th

OPPOSITE: Throughout its history, Paris has been known as a birthplace for new ideas and art forms. This was especially true of the early 1900s, when Parisian cafés were filled with artists discussing the new movement known as Cubism.

9

century, movements in art are the expression of a culture. Sometimes that expression is so powerful and compelling that it reaches through time to carry its message to another generation.

In a dimly lit corner of a Parisian café, a group of young artists have gathered to discuss ideas that are both radical and rebellious. It is the early 1900s, and these pioneers of abstraction are on the verge of developing Cubism—an artistic expression so revolutionary that many now consider it the most significant art movement of the 20th century, and perhaps the most pivotal movement in Western Art since the Renaissance. Although the movement lasted only from 1907 to the start of World War I in 1914, Cubism would forever change the way artists represented the world around them.

Era of Change

People living at the beginning
of the 20th century could feel
that change was in the air.
Major discoveries in science and
technology, advancements in
transportation—including the
first airplane flight—and the
increasing tensions caused by
imperialism were all setting the
stage for a new world era, and
artists of the time certainly sensed
it. Two artists who were profoundly

affected by these changes—Spaniard Pablo Picasso (1881–1973) and Frenchman Georges Braque (1882–1963)—reacted by developing a radical new artistic style known as Cubism. To fully understand the Cubist revolution and its wider effect on the art world, one must better understand the societal factors that led to its evolution.

The 20th century began at the peak of European power. Not only did European nations lead the world in scientific and technological knowledge, but they had accumulated the greatest material wealth by establishing colonial empires that spanned the entire globe. The African continent was divided between France, Britain, Germany, Italy, Belgium, Spain, and Portugal. Asia was also divided among the European world powers. Britain ruled India, Indonesia belonged to the Dutch, and France and Russia controlled great portions of the

Asian continent as well. In the Pacific Ocean, European nations ruled several colonies, while the U.S. controlled the islands of Hawaii and the Philippines.

These colonial empires were fueled by an imperialistic desire for the raw materials found in these faraway lands. But colonies also served as marketplaces for European goods. In addition, colonialism was driven by territorial expansion—the sheer desire to occupy more land. While this imperialism led to great economic success in Europe, it also led to increasing tensions and alliances between various nations that would eventually culminate in World War I in 1914.

In the years leading up to World War I, scientific discoveries rapidly changed the way people viewed the world around them. Radical new theories in physics shattered old notions of matter, space, and time. In addition to the theories of German physicists Albert Einstein (1879–1955) and Max Planck (1858–1947), Danish physicist Niels Bohr (1885–1962) introduced the atomic theory in 1913. Bohr's theory provided an entirely new model of the nuclear atom, officially ushering in the Atomic Age. The world was swiftly becoming dependent upon new forms of energy, encouraged by scientific discoveries that urged a desire for speed, dependence upon machines, and a frenzied drive to break the barriers of time and space.

Matter, Space, and Time

Europe stood at the forefront of scientific discovery in the early years of the 20th century. German physicist Max Planck introduced his quantum theory in 1900, which was followed in 1905 by Albert Einstein's (pictured) special theory of relativity. According to the quantum theory, atoms were no longer the smallest building blocks of matter but were in fact made up of even smaller building blocks—subatomic packets of energy called "quanta." Einstein's special theory, along with the general theory of relativity he introduced 10 years later, changed the stable, three-dimensional space of **Isaac Newton** into a shifting, four-dimensional model of space-time. The basic principles that people held to be true about the world were suddenly redefined.

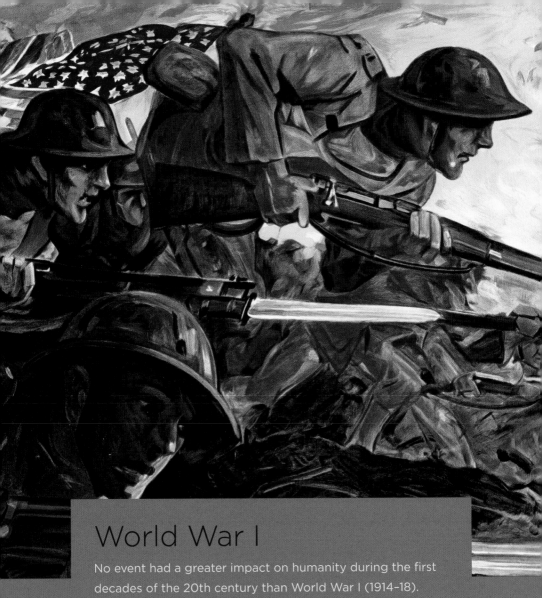

World War I

No event had a greater impact on humanity during the first decades of the 20th century than World War I (1914–18). European colonialism had led to nationalism, alliances, and political tensions that came to a violent head in 1914. Initially, Germany and Austria-Hungary fought against the allied countries of Britain, France, and Russia, who were later joined by the United States. Although many thought that the war would be over quickly, new technology and advancements in weaponry outpaced the existing tactics of war, resulting in drawn-out battles that left millions dead and many more wounded. After four years, Europe was left in ruins, and global power made a long-term shift to the U.S.

These new ideas shook the very foundation of what people had believed about the world since the 1600s and the Age of Enlightenment that followed. The solid, stable universe was now a shifting cosmos that challenged scientists to redefine theories that had been accepted for centuries as absolute truth. These new theories—along with the use of technology for mass destruction during World War I—shook the confidence that people had previously placed in science and reason and instilled newfound fears and doubts.

While science was leaving people on unsteady ground, the invention of the airplane enabled people to leave the ground behind them entirely. One of the most significant breakthroughs of the 20th century—the successful flight of American inventors Orville and Wilbur Wright in 1903—caused a variety of reactions. With the Wrights' success, the world would soon become a smaller place, as travel between distant nations was made faster and more efficient. The Wright brothers' historic feat also dramatically changed military tactics forever.

Besides exploring the wonder of flight and the inner workings of the atom, humankind was also exploring the depths of the human mind at the turn of the century. Swiss psychologist Carl Gustav Jung's (1875–1961) introduction of analytical psychology delved deep into the human unconscious, analyzing dreams, hallucinations, and fantasies to help people better understand their

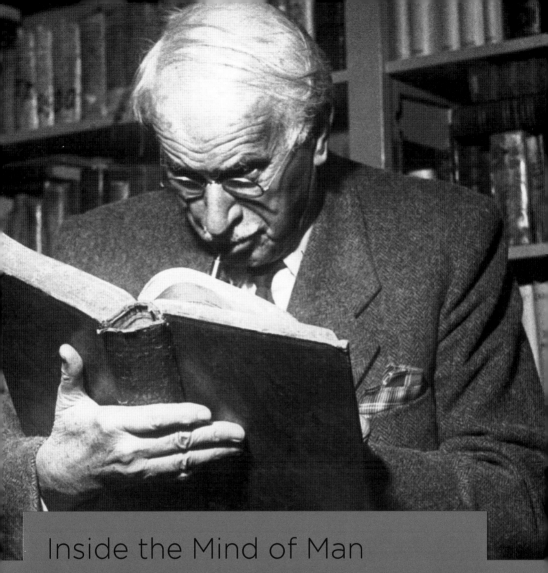

Inside the Mind of Man

The first years of the 20th century were marked not only by a desire to unravel the mysteries of the natural world, but also by a need to look inward and explore the human mind. One of the leaders in that field was Carl Gustav Jung, the father of modern psychology. Jung spent many years observing patients and recording their dreams, fantasies, delusions, and hallucinations. Through studying his data, Jung developed his theories of analytical psychology, which are still our broadest and most comprehensive views of the human **psyche**. A key portion of Jung's theories is focused on methods to understand a person's unconscious mind—the memories and thoughts of which people are not normally aware.

19

hidden fears and desires. Jung's analysis of the human psyche also attempted to counteract growing anxieties about a world in constant flux.

Within the city of Paris, France, these new theories and discoveries combined with unique urban factors to influence the development of the artistic avant-garde. Advances in industry and manufacturing since the Industrial Revolution in the late 1700s had led to the creation of a working class, and while this resulted in a booming economy, it also led to increased social disparity. While wealthy factory owners helped maintain the existing cultural hierarchy, the creation of a working class caused a shift in the primary audience for art. There was a growing demand for art that was created not only for the elite, as had been the case in the past, but also for the general public to enjoy. The creation of a new audience provided an ideal opportunity for the avant-garde to experiment with innovative ideas and techniques.

Beyond purely new techniques and ideas, however, many artists felt the need for an entirely new artistic style, an original form of visual expression that departed from the traditions set in place during the Renaissance. At the start of the 1900s, the world was facing a new era of uncertainty, and the pioneers of Modernism were seeking a new art that would convey that uncertain worldview.

BELOW While the fruits and other objects in Paul Cézanne's *Still Life With a Basket* (c. 1890–95) are easy to identify, he did not create them to look realistic but to serve as simple decorative objects instead.

The artistic groundwork for the birth of Cubism was laid in part by Paul Cézanne (1839–1906), a French painter who sought a style of painting that was more expressive in form and color than the Impressionists before him. His still lifes and landscapes painted during the late 19th century gave structure and intellectual order to the fleeting light and colors that dominated Impressionism. His focus was on the forms and shapes in nature, which, in his paintings, became stylized planes of color not tied to a photographic truth. In doing so, he reduced the importance of the subject matter and called attention to the painting itself and the qualities it possessed, independent of the subject.

At the turn of the century, a group of Parisian artists led by Henri Matisse (1869–1954) began working in a

Although Henri Matisse never fully adopted the techniques of Cubism, its influence can still be seen in his work, including *Portrait of Madame Matisse* (1913), in which the subject's face has lost its natural form, becoming mask-like.

style based mostly on pure color and raw emotion. After seeing some of their paintings at an exhibit in 1905, critics dubbed the artists *Les Fauves*, which means "wild beasts." Their style, while passionate and vibrant, did not last long. Many artists translated the vivid colors and bold brushstrokes into more personal styles, while others completely revolted against the stylistic elements of Fauvism, searching for a new artistic vocabulary that would better express the fleeting nature of the modern world. For Picasso, Braque, and their followers, Cubism became that language.

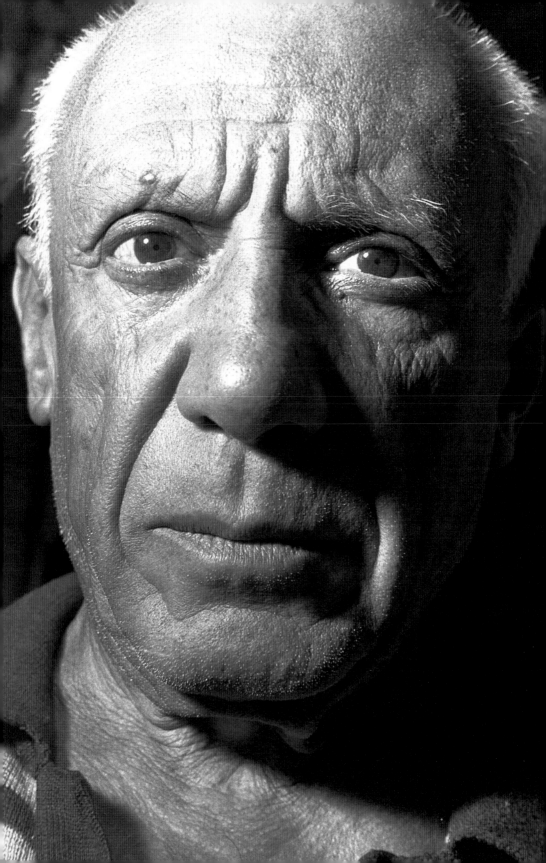

Cubist Artists

Originally from Málaga, Spain, Pablo Picasso mastered the technical aspects of late 19th-century realism by the end of the 1890s, even though he was only a teenager. While he followed traditional methods of drawing from live models and making numerous studies before each painting, his constant experimentation and switching between various styles was

OPPOSITE: Despite the fact that Picasso received only limited formal training in art, having left his college-level courses of study after less than a year, he quickly became one of the 20th century's most acclaimed and influential artists.

inherently modern. In 1900, Picasso went to Paris—the cultural center of the day—for the first time. He settled there permanently four years later.

Georges Braque was a housepainter's son who came to Paris in 1900 from his home in Le Havre, France. By 1906, Braque was a member of the colorful Fauves and frequently spent time with other young artists, including Picasso, at cafés in the city's Montmartre district. In 1907, Braque visited Picasso's studio for the first time. There, he saw a painting that Picasso had shown to only a few other friends and fellow artists: *Les Demoiselles d'Avignon* (1907). Although disgusted by the brutality and ugliness of the painting, Braque realized that his friend was on the verge of a revolutionary new approach to painting. Within eight months, Braque had painted his first canvas in the new style.

In a series of still lifes and landscapes painted in 1907 and 1908 in the French countryside, Braque merged the foreground and background to create a shifting space that was hard to decipher. When he returned to Paris, Braque showed his new paintings at the Salon, the most famous gallery for new art exhibits in all of Paris. After seeing the paintings, art critic Louis Vauxcelles commented that Braque had "reduced everything to cubes." From that point on, Braque, Picasso, and their followers were referred to as Cubists.

After Braque's visit to Picasso's studio in 1907, the two artists began working together to develop their new style, which began as a direct reaction against Fauvism. They ignored the issue of color and instead focused on form and structure. Unlike the color-rich canvases of the Fauves, the earliest Cubist works were mostly monochromatic. Picasso and Braque used simple shapes, breaking forms into a series of overlapping planes. Their paintings were based more on intellect than emotion, and the work they produced during those years became known as "Analytic Cubism."

In 1911, at the height of the Analytic phase, Picasso's work was almost indistinguishable from Braque's. Although both artists still intended for their paintings to be representational, they rejected the traditional belief that a painting should try to portray the world exactly as it appears. Instead, they sought less literal and more conceptual representations of their subjects. As a result, paintings from this time lack the elements of light, atmosphere, and space that give depth and richness to the natural world.

Picasso and Braque felt that the most accurate representation of reality in painting was one that revealed

multiple viewpoints of an object at the same time, since it presented a complete image of what people knew about the object in their minds. In order to produce a simultaneous representation, they "analyzed" objects into their basic elements of planes and angles and reassembled them in a shallow, ambiguous space. The fragments were overlapped into patterns that suggested the entirety of the object. Recognizable pieces of the subject—such as bits of text, the bridge of a guitar, or the label on a bottle—were also included on the canvas as clues to help the viewer understand the paintings.

By 1911, there was an entire school of Cubists in Paris that had adopted Picasso and Braque's ideas about painting. Although works by these Cubist "students" are considered secondary to those of the founding fathers of Cubism, the Paris school held an exhibit in 1911 that finally brought

Cubism to the Parisian public. This school was founded by Frenchman Jacques Villon (1875–1963), who first followed the Cubism of Picasso and Braque but eventually developed a style that was a bit less analytical. Villon made his studio in Puteaux the meeting place of the Parisian Cubists.

Albert Gleizes (1881–1953) and fellow French artist Jean Metzinger (1883–1956) were members of the Puteaux circle and together published a book on Cubist theory entitled *Du Cubisme* in 1912. Metzinger was first introduced to Cubism in 1907, shortly after the movement was conceived. He exhibited with the Parisian Cubists in 1911 at the Salon and joined the Puteaux group that year; Gleizes had already joined the Cubist movement two years earlier, in 1909.

One of the best-known members of the Parisian school was French artist Robert Delaunay (1885–1941).

Although he studied with the Puteaux artists, he was strongly influenced by Paul Cézanne and the Fauves. Through his use of vivid color, Delaunay developed his personal style into a completely abstract form of painting known as Orphism. His circular forms of 1912 were some of the first paintings to hint at pure abstraction, and the impact of his work spread far beyond Paris. His wife, Sonia Terk Delaunay (1885–1979), was an innovative artist in her own right, creating works in ceramics, quilting, and the textile arts that illustrated the influence of Cubism, Orphism, and Futurism.

French painter Fernand Leger (1881–1955) met Picasso and Braque in 1910. By 1912, he had developed a personal style that incorporated elements of Cubism and Purism. The Purist notion of art took elements of Cubism, such as the analysis of forms into basic shapes, and combined them with the simplified aesthetics of the machine age. During the war, Leger became fascinated with the beauty of mechanical forms. He developed a Purist form of Cubism based on the mechanized shapes of cylinders, cones, and gears, and used areas of broad, flat color to depict massive, robot-like figures in his paintings. His painting *The City* (1919) is indicative of his work in the representation of modern urban life.

Spanish artist Juan Gris (1887–1927) joined Picasso and Braque in 1911 and was the only other artist they accepted as a "true" Cubist. His style was quite intellectual, and he painted analytical works that were sophisticated and very geometrical, using bold bits of color. The unique Cubist style exhibited by Gris had a decidedly classical edge, with a more naturalistic and descriptive use of light and modeling.

Gris also contributed to the development of the second phase of Cubism—known as "Synthetic Cubism"—beginning in 1912. It was at this time, right after Analytic Cubism had reached its peak, that the movement experienced a key turning point. Instead of analyzing an object into its basic elements and reconstructing them on the canvas, Picasso, Braque, and their followers began to create paintings by attaching bits of newspaper, cloth, and other objects directly to the surface of the canvas, a technique known as collage.

The introduction of the collage process also renewed the Cubist interest in color and allowed artists to create spatial relationships without the use of traditional perspective. By fixing actual bits of objects onto the canvas, Cubists broke the two-dimensional nature of the picture

By fixing actual bits of objects onto the canvas, Cubists broke the two-dimensional nature of the picture plane.

plane. This allowed the viewer to focus on the painting as an actual object itself, as opposed to a window into another reality, which had been accepted since the Renaissance. This change in the relationship between the viewer and the canvas was another landmark in the history of Western painting.

Man Takes to the Skies

For hundreds of years, man had repeatedly tried and failed to create a flying machine. Then, on a cold winter morning in 1903, brothers Orville and Wilbur Wright accomplished just that. On December 17, at Kitty Hawk, North Carolina, the American aviation pioneers took their invention, the *Wright Flyer*, for a 120-foot (37 m) flight. Five years later, in the spring of 1908, human flight was introduced to Europe when Wilbur traveled to France to demonstrate the wonder of aviation. Over the next 12 months, he made more than 200 flights in France, Italy, and Germany.

Great Works of Cubism

The first painting created in the Cubist style—and the one that compelled Braque to join Picasso in the development of the Cubist movement—was Picasso's *Les Demoiselles d'Avignon* (1907). The painting is grand in scale, eight feet (2.5 m) tall and eight feet (2.5 m) wide, and the canvas is filled with the images of five female figures. The use of traditional

The use of traditional perspective is gone.... he broke the figures into jagged planes of color.

perspective is gone, and although Picasso used areas of light and shade, it was not to convey depth—another rejection of the Western tradition. Instead, he broke the figures into jagged planes of color.

In addition, the painting's fractured figures are seen from more than one location in space, particularly the figure in the lower right corner. The broken angles of her body seem to be viewed from the front, the side, and the back—a simultaneous and shattered perspective that questions the connection between time and space, one of the foundations of Cubist theory. Picasso's interest in primitive art is strikingly evident throughout the painting. The faces of the three women on the left show the

CUBISM

Like many of Gris's other pieces, *Coffee Grinder* (1920) focuses on subject matter from his immediate surroundings and is housed at Spain's Museo Nacional Centro de Arte Reina Sofía.

influence of Iberian carving, which Picasso saw while on summer visits to Spain, while the two figures on the right reflect the influence of the harsh angles of African masks.

The year after Picasso painted *Les Demoiselles*, Braque created a series of still lifes and landscapes that represented an even more mature development of the Cubist ideals. Drawing heavily from the influence of Cézanne, Braque's paintings of the French countryside near the city of L'Estaque go beyond the flattened planes of Cézanne's landscapes. In paintings such as

Road Near L'Estaque (1908), fragments of sky interplay with broken planes of green vegetation, earthy fields, and warm rooftops. Braque went a step farther than Cézanne in disregarding the physical laws of nature; light comes from conflicting sources, and the shifting space seems compressed within the two-dimensional surface of the canvas.

As Picasso and Braque worked together to develop the language of Cubism, their visual vocabularies became almost identical, especially at the height of Analytic Cubism. A telling example of this is Braque's *Man with a Guitar* from 1911 and Picasso's *The Accordionist* from the same year. At this stage of Cubism, color had lost its importance, and the palette had been reduced to a series of monochromatic browns and grays. In both paintings, the figures are almost impossible to discern

One of the earliest artists to adopt Cubism was Jacques Villon, brother of artist Marcel Duchamp. Although Villon's *Young Woman (Girl)* (1912) looks almost completely abstract, closer inspection reveals the outline of a female form. Its strong colors and angular shapes give the piece a distinct sensation of movement.

upon first glance. Instead, they have been dissected into geometric elements—angles, lines, arcs, and planes.

Instead of merely painting or drawing the figure from one position, Picasso and Braque analyzed the forms from every possible angle and combined them all into one pictorial whole. But to understand the whole and discover the figure among the fragments, the viewer must study the painting and look for clues to the subject. Large planes intersect to hint at the form of a man, a guitar, or another recognizable subject. At the same time, smaller shapes seem to float on the surface or slip into the background, creating an ambiguous, shifting space.

The viewer's perception of space was further complicated as Braque and Picasso continued to develop their Cubist style into its Synthetic period. The work that marked the beginning of this new period is

Picasso and Braque analyzed the forms from every possible angle and combined them all into one pictorial whole.

Picasso's *Still Life with Chair Caning* (1912). Painted on a piece of oilcloth imprinted with the pattern of a cane chair seat, the round-shaped artwork was framed with a piece of common rope. Brushstrokes over the cane pattern seem to hover on the surface of the canvas, creating the appearance of a sculptural relief as opposed to a two-dimensional painting. Remarkably, the abstracted still life appears to be sitting upon a realistic tray, made more prominent by the oval shape of the painting. By attaching the oilcloth and the rope to *Still Life with Chair Caning*, Picasso disposed of the last remnants of Western tradition, as the painting itself became an object in space rather than simply an illusionistic representation.

CUBISM

Although Picasso, Braque, and the early Cubists sought to create a new spatial relationship, they confined their ideas mostly to the two-dimensional realm. Soon after the peak of Analytic Cubism, some artists began using Cubist notions, such as Primitivism, to explore the three-dimensional world. Eventually, a new form of sculpture evolved that took its cue from Analytic Cubism by fracturing objects into planar forms and emphasizing the changing relationship of space and time. Going against the tradition of solid sculptures made from carved or molded forms, this new style of sculpture used separate pieces of material to build up one sculptural whole.

Although these new sculptural ideas were tested by Picasso with, for example, *Woman's Head* (1909), one of the most successful Cubist-inspired sculptors was Jaques Lipchitz (1891–1973). Lipchitz was born in Latvia but

Interest in the Primitive

Colonialism in Europe had a profound effect on artists at the beginning of the 20th century. Although people in African and Middle Eastern civilizations had been creating art for centuries, artists working in avant-garde styles around 1900 in the cultural centers of Europe were essentially discovering this primitive art for the first time. The art from these civilizations was very different from traditional European tastes and intrigued the avant-garde. Picasso and many of his contemporaries, including Henri Matisse, drew inspiration from the African masks and primitive sculptures. Picasso was interested in the barbaric quality and power of the sculptures, because they disregarded classical notions of beauty and emphasized simplified forms to create raw, emotional power.

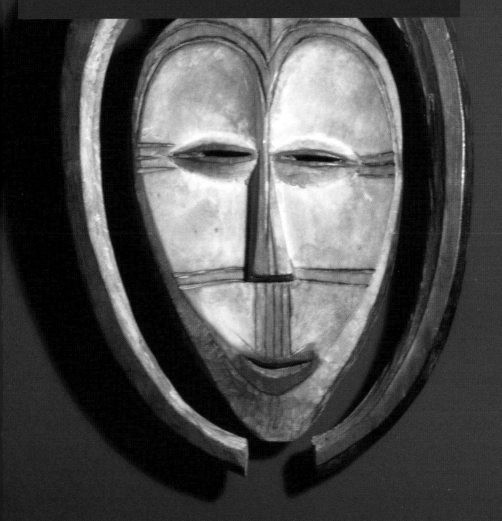

A second generation of Cubists ... took the innovations of Picasso and Braque to a more refined technical level ...

lived most of his life in France and the U.S. His *Bather* (1917) exhibits the continuous form of a figure broken into cubic volumes and planes that seem to slip and change before the eyes—playing on the new theories of modern physics. Lipchitz was part of a second generation of Cubists who took the innovations of Picasso and Braque to a more refined technical level, using proportion and mathematics to achieve their artistic goals.

French sculptor Henri Laurens (1885–1954) met Braque in 1911 and worked in a Cubist-inspired style between 1913 and 1925. He began creating "constructions"—assemblages much like collages—in 1913. A key example is *Woman in a Mantilla* (1918), which he exhibited at the Salon. Laurens later moved on to fully three-dimensional sculpture, including works such as *Man with a Clarinet* (1919) and *Head of a Young Girl* (1920).

Russian-born Parisian Alexander Archipenko (1887–1964) was also influenced by Cubist ideals. Following the example of Picasso and Braque, he broke with Western tradition and used holes in his sculptures, instead of projections, to represent solid objects. In *Woman Combing Her Hair* (1915), Archipenko used an empty

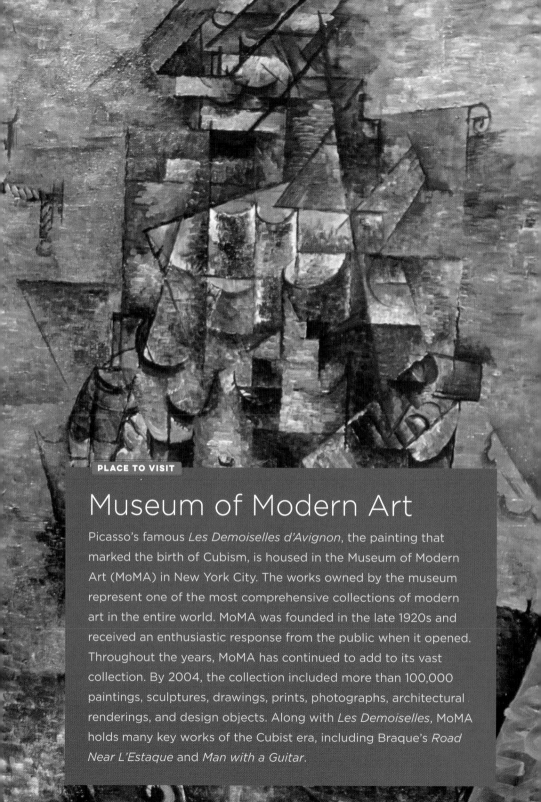

Museum of Modern Art

Picasso's famous *Les Demoiselles d'Avignon*, the painting that marked the birth of Cubism, is housed in the Museum of Modern Art (MoMA) in New York City. The works owned by the museum represent one of the most comprehensive collections of modern art in the entire world. MoMA was founded in the late 1920s and received an enthusiastic response from the public when it opened. Throughout the years, MoMA has continued to add to its vast collection. By 2004, the collection included more than 100,000 paintings, sculptures, drawings, prints, photographs, architectural renderings, and design objects. Along with *Les Demoiselles*, MoMA holds many key works of the Cubist era, including Braque's *Road Near L'Estaque* and *Man with a Guitar*.

void to represent the head, thereby turning a negative space into a reference for mass.

F

rench artist Raymond Duchamp-Villon (1876–1918) was one of the most significant sculptors of his time. In *Horse* (1914), one of his best-known works, he portrayed a near-perfect sculptural expression of animal and mechanical energy. His brother, Marcel Duchamp (1887–1968), worked in a dynamic vein of Analytic Cubism in 1911 and 1912. Considered a fringe artist even by the avant-garde, Duchamp's *Nude Descending a Staircase, No.* 2 (1912) caused a scandal at the Armory Show of modern art in New York City in 1913 because the painting went against all established notions of how people thought the nude figure should be represented.

Marcel Duchamp later delved into the realm of sculpture, taking cues from the Synthetic phase of Cubism. While collage techniques allowed art to be made from found objects, Duchamp set out to show that found objects could themselves be art. He accomplished this with his so-called "readymades," including the ordinary bottle rack that he determined to be a work of fine art in 1914. Duchamp believed that anything can be art if the artist decides it is. In essence, he decided that art is not in the making but in recognizing an object's aesthetic value.

A World Forever Changed

Between 1907 and 1914, Picasso and Braque shared an intense collaboration as they broke the accepted boundaries of Western art. But at the start of World War I in 1914, Braque and many Cubist followers enlisted in the French army, while Picasso, a **pacifist**, stayed out of the war. This dispersal of artists at the outset of the war signaled the end of the

Cubist movement. But Cubism had already left its mark on the artistic styles and ideologies of most avant-garde artists in Europe and beyond.

C ubism's use of raw forms and fragments opened the door for the complete abstraction that was to become the starting point for the development of modern art. Throughout the war years, the stylistic elements of Cubism remained very influential, and the movement stayed alive after World War I by helping to shape subsequent art movements. Indeed, much painting, sculpture, and architecture followed Cubism's path of influence, and today, the lasting effects of the Cubist movement on our world can be seen everywhere.

Even before World War I began, the Italian Futurists drew inspiration from the first phase of Analytic Cubism. Consumed with the spread of technology across Europe and people's increasing dependence upon the machine in industry, the followers of Futurism saw the geometric planes and forms of Cubism as a way of representing the dynamism of modern life. Italian artists such as Giacomo Balla (1871–1958) and Umberto Boccioni (1882–1916) used Cubist elements as a way to express intense speed and violent motion through shape and color.

Both Balla and Boccioni borrowed from Cubism's desire to represent objects through simultaneous views, especially objects in motion. Balla captured this simultaneity in his painting *Dynamism of a Dog on a Leash* (1912), in which he rendered both the legs and tail of the dog, along with the feet of its owner, as though the viewer were able to see their entire range of motion all at the same moment. In his *Dynamism of a Cyclist* (1913), Boccioni managed to likewise communicate the energy of pedaling a bicycle through Cubism's vocabulary. He also expressed the complexity of urban living by making his subject indistinguishable from its surroundings.

The effects of Cubism on Futurist ideals spread from the two-dimensional canvas into the realm of sculpture as well. On April 11, 1912, Boccioni published the *Technical Manifesto of Futurist Sculpture,* in which he demanded radical new kinds of sculpture and rejected tradition. He called for sculpture that used all sorts of materials and depicted energy, space, and relationships.

Boccioni published the *Technical Manifesto of Futurist Sculpture*, in which he demanded radical new kinds of sculpture ...

One of Boccioni's most famous pieces, *Unique Forms of Continuity in Space* (1913), is perhaps the definitive work of Futurist sculpture. In it, the effects of motion are illustrated in the space around the figure rather than on the figure itself. Drawing on the influence of Analytic Cubism, the figure is distinguishable only behind a blur of movement hinted at by expanded and contoured forms.

CUBISM

In keeping with Futurism's desire to portray speed and action, Boccioni's *Dynamism of a Cyclist* eliminates horizontals and verticals, instead emphasizing whirling lines and fusing the figure with its background.

Besides opening the door to abstraction in painting and sculpture, Cubism also strongly influenced architecture and the industrial arts. Modern architects took cues from Cubism to design contemporary skyscrapers with fragmented angles and intersecting planes, transforming the surroundings of everyday life through buildings designed with simple lines and a lack of ornamentation. The use of new materials, such as iron and steel, reinforced concrete, aluminum, plastics, and structural glass, helped to replace the accepted traditions of architecture with a new type of design that profoundly changed the way people think about buildings. Collage techniques introduced by the Cubists influenced the designs of innovative architects, from Le Corbusier (Charles Edouard Jeanneret, 1887–1965) and his Notre Dame du

Haut chapel (1955) at Ronchamp, France, to American architect Frank Gehry (1929–) and his Weisman Art Museum at the University of Minnesota (1990). Likewise, the earlier phase of Cubism influenced the work of architects such as Frank Lloyd Wright (1867–1959), one of the best-known and most prolific American architects.

The advent of Cubism and the beginning of abstract art also created a need for a new type of institution or venue to display the radical new artistic styles. In the 1920s, the Museum of Modern Art in New York City was founded by three influential arts patrons: Lillie P. Bliss, Mary Sullivan, and Blanchette Rockefeller. These forward-thinking women saw the need to create an institution unlike conventional museums, which tended to cater their space toward traditional Western art. Instead, they envisioned a museum with spaces specifically built

The way in which simple, geometric forms have been analyzed and reassembled in the design of the Weisman Art Museum shows the clear influence of Cubism on its architect, Frank Gehry.

Cubism's most important legacy is its breaking from Western art tradition, paving the way for an entirely new era of representation...

for the Modernist styles. When the museum opened its doors in 1929, modern art was given a new degree of legitimacy and recognition as the official art of the new period in history.

Frank Lloyd Wright agreed that a traditional museum was not suited for displaying such revolutionary art, and he set about designing a nontraditional space that would help viewers see art in new and different ways. In 1959, his design became reality, and the doors opened to the Solomon R. Guggenheim Museum (named in honor of its founder, a famous philanthropist). Since it first opened to the public, the New York museum has drawn huge crowds, pushed the boundaries of traditional notions of a museum, and stirred visitors with the power and excitement of its curving forms.

As the first manifestation of abstract art, Cubism's most important legacy is its breaking from Western art tradition, paving the way for an entirely new era of representation in painting and sculpture. Challenging longstanding notions of realism, Cubism brought painting to the peak of intellectualism. It demanded that the viewer use his or her knowledge and past experience of objects to assemble the fragmented canvas in his or her own mind.

Another lasting influence of Cubism is the introduction of the collage painting technique during the Synthetic Period. Breaking with the traditional treatment of a painting as a mirror or window, the Cubists acknowledged the surface of the canvas by fixing items to the paintings that defied the two-dimensional plane. Collage also challenged the purpose of art by using objects and materials from everyday life. Instead of reproducing the look of materials, they used the actual materials themselves. Picasso and Braque also confronted current ideas of reality in more complex and sophisticated ways by using collage materials to represent other objects, such as using newspaper in the shape of a bottle, a guitar, or a pipe.

Musée Picasso

The Musée Picasso, located in Paris, France, is home to *Still Life with Chair Caning*, one of the revolutionary paintings that signified the start of Synthetic Cubism. Founded two years after Picasso's death in 1973, the museum is housed in a 17th-century mansion that holds an impressive collection of Picasso's paintings, sculptures, collages, and drawings. In addition, the museum exhibits artwork gathered from the artist's own personal collection, including works by Braque. The pieces in the Musée Picasso are arranged chronologically, beginning with Picasso's *Self Portrait* (1901) and ending with *Old Man Seated* (1971). In this way, viewers can see Picasso's artistic progression, including the period of experimentation that led to the development of Cubism.

As the 20th century progressed, the Cubist disregard for the boundaries of traditional Western art allowed the continued exploration and questioning of accepted notions of fine art. From Dada to Pop Art to Post-Modernism, practically every artistic movement of the last 100 years owes a bit of its existence to Cubism. And although Picasso and Braque claimed that they were only satisfying their personal artistic interests, their radical way of approaching painting at the beginning of the 1900s redefined what art was expected to be. In essence, by breaking the rules of the day, Cubists made it possible for artists to express themselves openly and freely. Today, artists no longer need to adhere to a predetermined set of guidelines; there is no longer a "right" or "wrong" way to create art as there was before the Cubist revolution. And our world is a much more expressive and beautiful place because of it.

Solomon R. Guggenheim Museum

Some of the landmark paintings of the Cubist era can be found at the Solomon R. Guggenheim Museum in New York City. Founded in 1939, the museum was first known as the Museum of Non-Objective Painting. Upon the insistence of philanthropist Solomon Guggenheim, the museum focused on the exhibition of the work of artists who were developing radical new forms of art. Although the museum's first home was in a former automobile showroom on East 54th Street, its permanent home was later designed by American architect Frank Lloyd Wright. Still considered one of the greatest works of 20th-century architecture, the Guggenheim houses an array of Cubist masterpieces, including Picasso's *The Accordionist* and Delaunay's *Eiffel Tower* (1911).

GUGGEN

Timeline

1900   Max Planck introduces his quantum theory

Pablo Picasso visits Paris for the first time

Georges Braque moves to Paris

1903   The Wright Brothers make the first successful human flight

1904   Picasso settles in Paris

1905   Albert Einstein introduces his special theory of relativity

1907   Picasso paints *Les Demoiselles d'Avignon*

Braque visits Picasso's studio for the first time; they begin working together to develop a new style

1908   Braque paints a series of abstract landscapes; a critic coins the term "Cubism" after viewing them

1909   Albert Gleizes joins the Cubist movement

1910   Fernand Leger meets Picasso and Braque and begins developing his own Cubist style

1911   The peak of Analytic Cubism; Picasso's and Braque's works are almost identical

The Paris School of Cubists holds a public exhibition

Juan Gris joins Picasso and Braque

1912   Collage is introduced in Picasso's *Still Life with Chair Caning*, signaling the start of Synthetic Cubism

Jean Metzinger and Gleizes publish *Du Cubisme*, a book on Cubist theory

Umberto Boccioni publishes the *Technical Manifesto of Futurist Sculpture*

Robert Delauney paints his series of circular forms that hint at pure abstraction

1913　Niels Bohr introduces his atomic theory

Armory Show of modern art is held in New York City; Marcel Duchamp's *Nude* causes a scandal

Boccioni sculpts *Unique Forms of Continuity in Space*

1914　World War I begins

Braque enlists in the French army, and Cubist artists disperse

Raymond Duchamp-Villon sculpts his expressive *Horse*

Marcel Duchamp creates the first "readymade" with a bottle rack

1917　World War I ends

Bibliography

Cole, Bruce, and Adelheid Gealt. *Art of the Western World: From Ancient Greece to Post-Modernism*. New York: Simon & Schuster, 1989.

Gardner, Louise. *Art through the Ages*. Orlando, Fla.: Harcourt Brace, 1991.

Gilbert, Rita, and William McCarter. *Living with Art*. 2nd ed. New York: Knopf, 1985.

Janson, H. W., and Anthony F. Janson. *History of Art*. 6th ed. New York: Abrams, 2001.

Glossary

abstract   a type of art that does not depend on the realistic representation of objects, but rather on color, form, and other stylistic elements

Age of Enlightenment   a period in history beginning in the 1700s that was characterized by a strong faith in science and reason

atomic   describing a small particle of matter

avant-garde   a group of artists that worked to develop new techniques and styles during the 19th and 20th centuries

collage   a technique in which an artist attaches paper, rope, glass, or other objects to a two-dimensional canvas in layers

Dutch   people from the Netherlands, a country in northern Europe

Futurism   an artistic movement that was influenced by Cubism and drew influence from machines to depict movement, speed, and energy

Imperialism   the policy of a country extending its power by acquiring territory or establishing rule over another nation

Impressionists   a group of artists in the late 19th century who were interested in the quality of light on objects and the landscape

Isaac Newton	a scientist (1642–1727) who developed the theory of gravity and the laws of motion, force, and velocity that were considered absolute truth until the 20th century
Modernism	the period in art history that includes Cubism, usually thought of as beginning in the late 19th to early 20th centuries
Orphism	a completely abstract form of painting based mainly on form and color
pacifist	a person who objects to war and refuses to serve in the military
philanthropist	a person who promotes human welfare, often through acts or donations of charity
psyche	the human mind and its thoughts, feelings, and emotions, as separate from the physical body
Purism	a movement begun by painter and architect Le Corbusier based on Cubist ideals and machine aesthetics
relief	describing sculpture that projects slightly from a flat surface
Renaissance	a period of artistic and cultural rebirth and discovery in European history that began in the late 15th century
unconscious	the thoughts and mental processes of which a person is not actively aware, such as dreams

Index